Everything Else Is Bric-a-Brac

Everything Else Is Bric-a-Brac

Notes on Home

Akiko Busch

Illustrations by

Aurore de la Morinerie

PRINCETON ARCHITECTURAL PRESS · NEW YORK

*When I say the first line of the Lord's
Prayer, 'Our father who art in heaven,'
I imagine this heaven as invisible,
unenterable but intimately close. There
is nothing baroque about it, no swirling
infinite space or stunning foreshortening.
To find it—if one had the grace—it would
only be necessary to lift up something as
small and at hand as a pebble or a salt-
cellar on the table.*

—JOHN BERGER

Question your teaspoons.

—GEORGES PEREC

Contents

Preface

Some years ago, I wrote a collection of essays called *Geography of Home*. I was interested then in our public and private lives, our memories of and aspirations toward home, and how our ideas about domestic space reflect our thoughts about society, culture, the natural environment. And how we search out comfort, privacy, security. The collection of short prose pieces here follows up on some of these ideas, though these look instead to the ambiguities that can be generated by ideas of home. They are more likely to read as leaflets on the uncertainties of domestic life; on ideas of placement and displacement; on the frailty and tenacity of human memory; on the beauty of use and uselessness alike; and how we do—and don't—find our place in the world. Which is to say, if these short pieces are about being settled, they are also about being *unsettled*.

The distractions, missteps, miscalculations we experience at home can move us to identify discontents. And a sense of displacement can define something real. It seemed odd to me that while this realm of experience, sometimes even the abiding *value* of this realm of experience, may

appear in fiction, memoirs, biographies, and poetry,
it is addressed less often in the archives of design writing.
Still, it is common to human considerations of the material world—in the deliberate imperfection in Navajo
weaving that serves as the spirit path for the weaver; in the
cracked bowl of the Japanese potter reflecting the wabi-
sabi belief that nothing lasts, everything changes, nothing
is perfect; in the misplaced patch of color in an Islamic
rug, a reminder that human beings always fall short; in the
flaw of an Amish quilt that is intended to reflect humility.
But wait! That last one is a myth, I learned. Someone
made it up! A lie!

Such errors, and errors about errors, are crucial to the
way we live; they are all part of the way we find meaning
in experience. Places come alive for us in myriad ways,
as in the angle of sunlight falling through the window, say,
or in the way a beat-up kitchen table conveys a sense of
sufficiency. But rooms come to life in other ways as well:
a desk next to a cold window in winter; an immovable
piece of furniture; a decal on a child's window; the danger
inherent in an electric fan or in a pressure cooker; a fireplace that has been boarded up and appears to be useless.
How we remember places, rooms, and the things in them
may be as flawed as the way we remember anything else,
but such defective memories have meaning too. I am

interested in such breaks in pattern, the missing thread, the lost stitch, the loosened tile, the splinter in the floor-board, the lie of the quilt, and the possible grace that might be offered by such small flaws and inadequacies.

Festival

When I was a very young child, one of my favorite books was *Mei Li*. Written and illustrated in the 1930s by an American graphic artist named Thomas Handforth, it told the story of a young girl in rural North China. Her confinement is explicit. The house is covered in snow and surrounded by a wall, and girls are meant to stay at home. All the same, Mei Li sneaks out one morning with her brother, hops on an ice sled, and attends the New Year's celebration in the nearby city.

There she encounters a palace, a toy shop, a bell tower, a bridge of wealth. She spends a penny on firecrackers. She sees girls walking on stilts, encounters a bear doing tricks, dances on the back of a Mongol circus pony, encounters a priest who, in exchange for her coral-red marble, predicts that she will rule over a kingdom. At story's end, she is both exhilarated and exhausted and returns home on the back of a camel barely in time to meet the Kitchen God. Appearing through the smoke and flame of incense, he tells the small girl that it is her own household that will be her empire.

Looking back over this now, I see of course that there are countless ways to read this story. A saga of gender discrimination; a narrative of cultural appropriation; a lens on a patriarchal culture that demeans females; a westerner's condescending social perspective of Asian tradition; and so on. I Googled Handforth and learned that he was a shy graphic designer with a lifelong interest in Asian art. He traveled to China on a Guggenheim Fellowship, expecting only to spend a few weeks there, and ended up staying for six years. He took up lithography, which he felt was the correct medium with which to transcribe daily Chinese life. And it was during that time that he encountered a spirited four-year-old girl named Mei Li, the model for his heroine.

One of the curious things about *Mei Li* is that the action, such as it is, takes place at the festival: the priest under the pine tree, acrobatic girls who can throw pots and pans with their feet, a kite in the shape of a hawk, lanterns that look like fish. But when Mei Li finally arrives home and is told by the Kitchen God that her kingdom will be her own household, its dimensions are left unclear. Her dominion remains a mystery. There is no parallel drama or picturesque imagery, unless you consider the honey cakes and dumplings with which her mother has summoned the Kitchen God.

Today you might read that as some clever postmodern literary device in which the untold and unknown story manages to convey the same weight and interest as that story that *is* told. But I doubt it. I suspect instead Thomas Handforth was just one of those writers who knew that what is said in a story can sometimes be balanced by what is unsaid.

In any case, Mei Li is curious, observant, resourceful, nervy, and even the youngest readers are left with the impression that she has the imagination to recognize the richness that makes up her own sovereignty. It is an indefinite and uncertain territory with imprecise borders, unclear systems, and unknown rewards. That fact interested me then, and it continues to interest me now.

Note

Not long ago, my husband and I arrived home to find
a message from our neighbor tacked on the door: "Hey—
Half-grown black bear in our yard. Friday, about 6:00 pm.
Headed in your direction —Tillman." The bear never showed
up, but I was so taken with this note that I framed it and hung
it on the doorframe where it remains today. In part, it was
the sense of anticipation it generated; just seeing it every time
I came home had me imagining that a black bear might stroll
into the yard at any moment. But as the months passed, I came
to realize it was more than that. The place we live is at the
edge of the woods at the bottom of a mountain, and in less
than twenty words, the little memo reminds me several times
a day of all the things headed in our direction that I will never
see and never know.

Waves

It was a late summer afternoon and we were on a boat,
this woman and I. She had just finished renovating her
house and was telling me about the granite countertops,
the beadboard cabinetry, the Italian tiles in the kitchen.
It was clear she had a good eye for design and had made
her decisions about furnishings and layout carefully.
She told me decisively that she would never have a televi-
sion in the bedroom, that this could destroy a marriage.
At the time, I thought I understood what she meant and
was surprised six months later to hear that she and her
husband had filed for divorce. I think back to this conversation and wonder, did she honestly believe that a TV in the
bedroom could kill a relationship? Or did she already antic-
ipate the coming break and see it everywhere, imagining
it even in the arrangement of an appliance, a piece of furniture. I realize now it was one of those brief exchanges in
which you have no idea what was actually being said, the
words and ideas as tenuous as the small boat bobbing along
the afternoon whitecaps as it heads toward the dock.

Tot Finder

Window treatments aren't a big thing here in our house in the Hudson Valley. A few linen curtains are about as far as it goes. We live in a rural area, and the unobstructed view to the outdoors works out pretty well. One bedroom upstairs is an exception to this, not that you'd really call what we've done a window treatment. Or maybe you would. Certainly it reframes the view. But it's really more like a window adhesive, which, at the moment, I am trying to scrub off. It's the tot finder decal we stuck on our two boys' bedroom window years ago when they were infants.

The shiny little silver and red mylar decal features a fireman, identified by the silhouette of his iconic hat, cradling an infant in his arms. It is a carefully crafted image of child protection meant to be fastened to the child's bedroom window, where it could alert the emergency rescue squad as to the whereabouts of small children in the event of a fire. But no sooner did we stick the thing on the window than its ambiguities were brought to our attention. Almost as quickly as local ladder companies passed these stickers out, they also began to advise parents to fasten them to the outside of the child's bedroom door instead. As it turns out, decals on children's bedroom windows are also sometimes regarded as targets by sexual predators.

In our country setting, I was never worried much about such predators climbing up to the roof and through the upstairs window. But the shiny little emblem for child safety that morphed into an advertisement for abuse became, in the end, an insignia for the impossibly elusive idea of child safety. Like the peanut butter sandwich that sends the kid into convulsions, the homegrown weed that one woman I know thought kept her teenager away from street drugs, or the Nest smart security camera that can be infiltrated by hackers spewing threats. And the fact that all those ingenious strategies we devise to make our kids safe can turn out to be just the ones that imperil them. So there it remained for some twenty-five years, a four-by-six-inch window treatment nonetheless loaded with contradictory meanings.

The boys are grown and have long since left these rooms. I think of all this as I try to scrape the decal off the window now. It is almost impossible to remove. The process requires soaking it with dish soap and hot water, peeling it off with a razor blade in a confetti of tiny scraps,

scrubbing the residue of calcified glue left behind without
scratching or cracking the glass, and then polishing
the pane one last time until it is completely transparent
and tells me nothing at all.

Garden Party

A faint diagonal scar runs down the middle finger of my
right hand between the second and third joint, a remnant of
an incident that occurred when I was four. It was late afternoon. Thirsty and tired, I asked my mother if I could have
a glass of lemonade. No, she said, it was too close to dinner
time. In a fit of toddler fury, I took the pitcher of lemonade
out of the refrigerator myself, found a cup, then smashed the
cup onto the surface of the glass table. This was before the
days of safety glass, and so the tabletop shattered, the cup
broke, the pitcher fell, and my hand was bleeding everywhere.

I see those wrought-iron and glass tables all the time.
It's garden furniture you find on patios and porches, but
indoors in dining rooms and restaurants too. The chairs and
table frame have delicate floral designs—little curlicues,
sprigs of laurel, roses, and hearts. The glass tabletop reflects
the light, the shadows of the leaves, the gleam of silver cutlery.
It is always a pretty arrangement, but one that also reminds
me of the way that fusion of human anger, sudden violence,
and material objects can be a part of our lives from nearly
the beginning.

Blueprint

When I was small, my father tried to give me a lesson in earth sciences. Using a lead cylinder with a pointed tip suspended from a piece of string, he made a plumb line. He told me, as I held the metal weight, that it was directed at the center of the earth. Trying to explain the idea of a vertical axis to a child, he also made a drawing of a girl in stick figure perched at a precarious angle on a circle representing the earth. She was holding the string with the weight that was directed toward the middle of the circle.

A simple diagram for the center of gravity, the picture made it clear. Yet it was impossible to understand. Maybe it was just my first experience with that distance between abstract thinking and real life, but when I think back to standing there, holding the piece of string with the cylinder dangling over the wood floor in a room with grass cloth on the walls inside a pastel-colored house in the Richmond District of San Francisco, trying to fathom how this could possibly be the center of the world, I am amazed that any of us ever manages to understand our place in things.

The Winter Desk

In the way that some people have lawn furniture or
a summer house, I have a winter desk. It is situated near
the window in a small upstairs bedroom, and I use it in
the cold months when I feel housebound. My son built the
desk in days when things were up in the air with him, the
circumstances of his life vague and undecided, and when
building material objects offered a visceral satisfaction.

He made it out of black walnut, but its honeyed grains
seem warmer than that, and when the snow weighs down
the branches of the white pine just outside the window,
the liquid patterns of the wood surface speak to the certainty of an eventual thaw. Which means it is a good place
to work. Especially when the thin January light filters
through the ice crystals on the panes of glass and onto the
fluid graphics of the wood grain, I think of what I would
like to tell my son, which is that it is possible for things to
be still and to move at the same time.

Exile

My friend and I are sitting across from each other in the museum café. We have just looked at an exhibition of paintings by the British artist John Constable, clouds and trees and rolling fields of the English countryside. "The sound of water escaping from mill-dams, willows, old rotten planks, slimy posts, and brickwork, I love such things," he said once.

My friend and I have known each other for more than forty-five years, and we are telling each other stories. We are talking about the paintings, our lives, books, people we know. And she says to me that she awoke that morning thinking about three houses: a house where she was once a caretaker; a friend's house in Massachusetts; and the house in which she lived in Vermont for three years with her husband to whom she is no longer married.

I don't know why it is that I remember these rooms so well, she tells me. But I remember them viscerally, physically. I remember how it felt to stand at the sink running the water, or to pull open the drawer of a desk, or the angle of the sunlight as it fell across the kitchen floor in the house in Vermont. I remember the feel of these rooms much more than I even remember the people in them. I can just recall their faces, but it is the rooms that I remember with the most detail.

And I suggest to her that it is possibly because remembering the people associated with those rooms may be so difficult. A friend who is no longer a friend, a lover with whom intimacy has passed. And she says, Maybe that's it. But I'm not sure it is. I think I remember those places, she says, because they are the rooms that are forbidden to me now. I know these rooms continue to exist, but I will never be in them again.

And this is something that perplexes me. We spend our time and money trying to make the places in which we live accommodating, open, and gracious. We desire the rooms we live in to be hospitable and human, and we do what we can to make them so. But in the end, it may be those that remain forbidden to us that we remember most clearly, the ones from which we are exiled that may fasten themselves most tenaciously to our memory and imagination.

Damage

I heard recently of two pastimes having to do with household goods that engage people today. The first is an emerging trend in some urban areas in which people pay to smash household objects with bats, crowbars, sledgehammers. The expression of rage is liberating, the thinking goes, and the demolition of crockery, televisions sets, and computer monitors in a controlled environment can be cathartic. The other is the revival of interest in the ancient Japanese art of kintsugi, the practice of repairing broken pottery by filling the cracks with a lacquer dust powdered with gold or silver, and therein learning to honor the rupture, the break, the scar.

What is interesting to me is not that these two opposite impulses have captured the popular imagination at the same time. It's no revelation that domestic objects can be the subjects of both rage and repair. I know that I have thrown glasses, slammed doors, and kicked baseboards myself. Who hasn't? And if I haven't filled the cracks in my own plates and bowls with powdered gold, I have sanded down scratches in our dining table with a sense of near devotion, and value to this day a chipped platter in my kitchen cabinet for its lifetime of accumulated imperfections.

What's more curious to me is the manner in which these two very different enterprises are practiced. Wrecking clubs and rage rooms where people pay to smash appliances, furniture, and utensils are offered as activities for date night, a kind of performative social event and something to do, apparently, with a person in whom one has some romantic interest or attachment. Kintsugi, though, is taught in workshop settings, a discipline to be practiced in more solitary surroundings. And this is the thing I am curious about: Why is it that destroying things is an activity to share with someone you love, while repairing things is done alone?

Rewards

Who knows exactly how we come to attach meaning to physical objects. Financial value, emotional associations, the circumstances of acquisition, the vagaries of human desire— all of these may come into it, but I know in my own life green stamps were involved as well. Part of a rewards program established by Sperry & Hutchinson in the middle of the last century, S&H Green Stamps were an early iteration of what we today call customer loyalty programs. The crisp sheets of green stamps, handed out at gas stations and supermarkets in the sixties and seventies, were then pasted into booklets that were later traded in at redemption centers for all manner of household goods.

The program's catalog, called an *Ideabook* (some of which can be found on eBay today), itemized the things offered: portable hairdryers, punch bowls, canisters, and beverage sets. But what I remember more than the things was the process. You licked the stamps then lined them up, square by square, to paste them into the grid of each page, to fill up the little booklets. There was something about the physical transaction that seemed to speak to how we attach ourselves to things; and the idea that the desire for things is something that could be quantified; and that worth arrives in increments, one little rectangle at a time. With all its implications of transit and delivery, of destination and arrival, the very idea of a stamp also conveyed a sense of promise and anticipation. Two more pages = a transistor radio!

To a child, the whole operation seemed haphazard. The terms of the exchange seemed obscure, the aggregates of value random and undefined. Three books of stamps might get you a toaster, five books a blender. Or maybe it was the reverse. Who knows. Because what it spoke to most of all was the fact that the way we attach value to things is both impossibly arbitrary and very, very precisely measured.

History

He was a friend of our parents and was doing research
at Stanford then, I think, and when he came to our house in
San Francisco he always brought me and my sister a box
of Russian jelly candies. I remember liking the orange ones
the most. Years passed, and then when I was eleven or twelve
I remember seeing him often at the house on East 91st
Street where we stayed when we went to Manhattan. It was
owned by a widow named Helen Simpson, whose husband
had been a congressman. Mr. Kerensky, as he was called,
was a permanent houseguest there. In the late afternoon,
my mother sat with him in the library, and because he
was all but blind, she read the newspaper to him, sentence
by sentence, cutting it up for him in little bites. He retained
a great interest in world affairs. Later, at dinner, Mr.
Kerensky sat at one end of the table and Mrs. Simpson at
the other. Because she was deaf, guests passed handwritten
notes up and down the table during the meal to keep the
conversation flowing. The dining table itself was a gigantic
white Parsons table, with a dark blue glass inlaid surface.
A Calder mobile fluttered above it all.

The blind revolutionary, the deaf hostess, the notes, the Calder—all of these remain vivid in my memory and imagination. It seems funny to me that I cannot now remember what we ate, the taste or aromas of the food that was served. I can recall none of those ephemeral things that are said to fasten experience to human memory. What I remember, instead, are the coordinates of those evenings—that is, the objects: the little white notepads, the black shards of the mobile, the blue ocean of the glass surface, the small white ceramic swans set at each place, even mine, filled with cigarettes fanned out to form the tail feathers of the swan. At that time, the fact that I was offered a swan full of cigarettes was more amazing to me than the fact that I was sitting at a table with Alexander Kerensky, a man who had almost changed the course of world history, but such a confusion about the facts is not unusual, I now know.

Home Advantage

What's called the "home advantage" is a phenomenon well-known in sports: teams playing on the home field—or court or rink—come to the game with a built-in lead. Whether it has to do with sleeping in their own beds, eating their own food in their own kitchens, or having the support of their fans in the bleachers, athletes seem to benefit from the supposed comforts of home.

The thing about this, though, is that it is a myth. Sports statisticians have found that playing at home is not always the boost it is assumed to be. In fact, athletes in different sports respond to the home advantage differently. While scores suggest that basketball players have an innate appreciation for home-stadium games, football and baseball players are less receptive to this presumed benefit. Of even greater interest is the fact that in critical games—that is, those games that determine season championships—athletes often falter when playing at home.

I wonder about this. Maybe if I could figure out why basketball players value the home advantage more than baseball players, or why athletes so often fumble in decisive contests at home, I would understand something more about the fine points of home advantage. What I suspect, though, is that home advantage can turn to disadvantage in the blink of an eye, and that the doubts cast around the idea of home advantage simply reflect the wider ambivalence so many of us have about this idea of home. Because just as surely as home can be a place of comfort, familiarity, and refuge, a place where our deepest social bonds are forged, at other times it can just as certainly be a place of divisiveness, anxiety, and uncertainty, a place where those same bonds can be stretched, diluted, and frayed beyond recognition.

Art

In the house I grew up in, a print hung in the kitchen for most of my teenage years. It was a silkscreen image called *Woman Reading* by the artist Will Barnet. The composition is simple: a direct, frontal view of a woman lying in bed under a red blanket holding a blue book. She has black hair in a blunt cut and is leaning against a white pillow; the wall behind her is green. There is a geometric plainness to the image, its blocks of color and simple shapes of bed, book, pillow, interrupted only by the rounded shape of a huge white cat lying on the woman's stomach. In our kitchen, the print hung above the white cube of the washing machine that only underscored its geometry.

I know my mother bought the print because she saw herself in it, and of course, we did too. The woman in the print looked a great deal like my mother right down to the short cropped dark hair. My mother also read books in bed late into the night and we had a huge white cat as well. In the print, the woman's eyes are visible just below the bottom edge of the book, yet for such a clear, direct image, it is not quite certain whether she is looking at the words on the page, or out of the print at the viewer, or out toward someplace even more distant. As with so many great portraits, the gaze is ambiguous.

The woman, the book, that cat—it was an image of stillness and composure, a portrait of her private being. That may be why years later, when I happened to see this print hanging in a gallery in Manhattan, I felt as though I had been gut-punched. In the kitchen, the thirty-by-forty-inch print was a window into her solitude, but in the art gallery, it was a wider exposure of an intimate family truth that had nothing to do with distance or remoteness, and everything to do with a woman being away as people in families often are.

Edges

It is an early March morning, the edge of a new season, and even the lake is a study of shifting parts. The half or so that remains ice is a dull gray slab, solid, while the half that the afternoon sun has lately managed to reach is dark water, brackish and unreadable. The gentle curve of their demarcation—drawn by some mysterious physics that takes in the angle of sunlight, the motion of current, the depth of water—thaws by the minute.

The transitions of the season are also playing out in a grassy field a quarter of a mile from the pond, where I see a porcupine lurching out of the woods. Nocturnal beings, they rarely appear in daylight, and I know that they ordinarily prefer to remain concealed in the shadows of their dens, hidden in the burrows and hollows of the woods, covered by the branches of shrubbery and trees. The disorientation of this one is clear, its long, light-colored guard hairs fanning out across its back, its haunches in an irregular, quivering wave, and beneath those, the white tips of its quills catching splinters of new spring light.

And if there is no telling why it happens to be here, it stumbles on, hesitant in its response to the daylight, to the wide, open space, to humans. Shapeshifting with every step, as though that might be enough to accommodate the light, the warmth, the new season, this little mascot of displacement is a study in asymmetry that reminds me how dislocation is a matter of fluid borders, one that looks to the inconstant thresholds of time and place alike.

Never

When I was ten I was given a book called *I Never Saw
Another Butterfly*. It was a collection of poems and
drawings made in the early 1940s by children imprisoned
at Terezín, a ghetto and concentration camp in Czech-
oslovakia. The cover of the book had a pretty drawing
made by one of the children: a yellow house with a red
roof and a circle of little spikes around the house signaling
a fence, black smoke pouring out of the chimney, green
mountains in the background.

I was told when I was given the book that most of
these children had died, either from disease and malnu-
trition at Terezín or later, after being sent to other exter-
mination camps. But at that age, it was not something
I could understand. Although the book was right in front
of me, this was something completely outside of my imagination, and it remained abstract knowledge. So I read the
poems and looked at the pictures. A poem about a little
mouse with fleas. Another one about tears. A picture of a
man in a boat sailing to Morocco.

Looking back now, I realize that this was when it first came to me that there is a difference between something making an impression on you and your actual grasp of the facts. And that sometimes the most we can know about something lies in the possibility that we may never comprehend it.

Things

I remember a postcard I once got from my mother. In less than fifty words she had described how she'd backed her car out of the garage, suddenly seen flames emerging from its engine, then was stilled by the decision of whether to rescue her handbag and tuna sandwich before she jumped out of the vehicle to call the fire department.

But I have learned it is common to be preoccupied by the quotidian in moments of catastrophe. In crisis, the mind focuses on the ordinary. Which is why, when a plane crashes on the runway, passengers often try to gather their belongings before racing to emergency exits. It may violate every rule of airline safety, yet people reach for their coats, phones, pillows, pens, laptops. Even though it may put our lives and those of others in peril, we instinctively turn to mundane things when confronted by disaster, valuing that way in which ordinary things can elicit ordinary thinking, an underappreciated frame of mind, perhaps, but sometimes one worth aspiring to.

Bounce House

When my husband and I moved into our farmhouse more than thirty years ago, it was its scale, the antique layout of rooms, the twelve-over-twelve windows, and the wide chestnut floorboards that all sparked my imagination. This sense of history matters to me still, but in the years since, I find my ideas about home now look to other models. Or rather, that there are other housing prototypes that seem more useful to me now. What's odd is that these other houses have been designed to engage children, and what's even more strange about these building types is that the ideas they project are not about comfort or security, but about disquiet and fear.

As a child I had a treehouse. Furnished with a small green chair with a straw seat and a low table with a red Formica top that had been fashioned from a piece left over from my mother's kitchen counter, it was positioned in the crook of an old maple tree. Its floorboards were fastened to branches that shuddered in the wind. Just as memorable was an octagonal glass house at an animal sanctuary I visited when I was ten. The interior walls—also transparent—

were only partial walls, but for the most part the interior was wide open. Inside was a reticulated python that was stretched from room to room, winding through the entirety of the glass house; it occupied every room, and the children walked around this house, staring into it, examining how the snake's body inhabited different spaces. Many years later, when a woman I knew described the atmosphere in her house during the time her daughter was addicted to heroin by saying "It felt as though a huge snake had wrapped itself around our house in a stranglehold," I was certain she had visited the same wildlife park as a child.

And then there is the playhouse for kids often called a bounce house. A little inflatable cabin, it is constructed of PVC vinyl and anchored to the ground with sandbags. It can be specified to resemble a cottage or a castle, and comes equipped with columns and turrets, a trampoline, piped-in music, and even a little swimming pool. Despite such amenities, what makes it most real to me is that if its anchors are insufficient, the house will tumble and blow across the landscape. A particularly strong gust of wind can sometimes even carry it into the clouds and away.

Family Dinner

I've noticed that contemporary restaurants increasingly favor what is thought of as family-style dining. These meals are informal affairs, with large bowls of food put directly on the table, diners sitting in close proximity, and friendly, though unceremonious, service. The rugs might be a little threadbare, the lighting soft. Conversation, often personal and spontaneous, is generated in a setting that is comfortable, if a little crowded.

It makes sense, these communal meals. The acceleration of family life, people's hectic schedules, and the availability of fast food and take-out meals all make it difficult for families to break bread together. Why not create the impression of a relaxed family dinner in a restaurant? And so people of all ages converge, bowls of risotto and platters of roasted vegetables are casually passed, and a sense of intimacy is established around a slightly scuffed oak or pine table. But honestly, maybe what makes these events most like a family meal is the way it is possible, suddenly and unexpectedly, to find yourself at the dinner table seated beside a complete stranger.

Work

I read recently that the Roomba robotic vacuum cleaner that started sweeping up homes in 2002 is the most commercially successful example of home technology. Nothing else—washing machines that chat with the stove, refrigerators that order the chardonnay, blinds that can be programmed to open at 8:00 a.m.—none of these come close, and they are generally greeted as novelty items that no one much cares about.

Which makes sense to me. People do things at home—they wash dishes, watch movies, take showers, roast chicken. But more important than any of these are the things we don't do. Gaze out the window with indifference. Walk into one room, then another, for no good reason. Stare at the ceiling. Listen to the traffic. Sit at the kitchen table for forty-five minutes drinking a cup of coffee. Home is a place where we can do things without purpose, without meaning, without motivation. And where aimlessness has its own meaning and use.

The French essayist Georges Perec has written about the need and value for a useless room, a functionless space that "would serve for nothing, relate to nothing," a void that even language is "unsuited to describing." And he tells us how it is possible, sometimes, for him to think of nothing. For all the talk about how new technologies and AI are going to reinvent the relationship between human behavior and what happens at home, I can't see how any of that will happen until there is some acknowledgment that home is a place where there is established value in doing and thinking and saying nothing at all.

Pressure Cooker

I am standing in a room with several hundred other people, and we are listening to a girl talk about cooking. This takes place on a college campus, and the meeting is about inclusion. So all of us—students, teachers, administrative staff—are listening to the girl from India who is telling us how she sometimes uses the dormitory kitchen to prepare the Indian food that gives her solace during these months when she is on the other side of the world from her home, family, and friends. She often uses a pressure cooker. Preparing these meals is something she enjoys doing, she tells us. It gives her comfort, so it didn't help when another student came into the dorm kitchen one evening and saw her fixing her meal. "Wow," the boy said. "A pressure cooker. That thing looks scary. No wonder it's what the Boston bombers used." When she repeated these words, a collective gasp went through the room.

I don't know who the boy was or where he came from. Maybe it was Connecticut or Texas or California. But it is easy to believe that his own parents did not use a pressure cooker. And that the collection of appliances in his own parents' kitchen more likely included an automatic espresso machine or a stainless steel bread maker. It is also easy to believe that his immediate connotations with that particular kitchen accessory did not have to do with the comforts of a homecooked meal, but with the apprehensions around a homemade bomb.

Maybe this encounter *is* about the visceral loneliness of an international student. Or maybe it *is* about the callous indifference of an American student. But what I think it is about, speaking of inclusion, is the way mundane household utensils come loaded with emotional meaning, associations, and values that are about as distant from each other as the continents and cultures they come from.

Housework I

I have been hearing a lot lately about how people are outsourcing domestic tasks, whether it is to gig economy housecleaners, robotic lawnmowers, or digital assistants. Household chores are supposed to be a source of dissatisfaction, especially in marriages; in one study, 25 percent of people filing for divorce stated the division of such labor as laundry, vacuuming, and washing the dishes as among the causes. One headline even said that families were happier when robots did the housework.

I'm not so sure. When she was a teenager, my friend Carin used to eavesdrop on her mother and her friends while they were sitting round the kitchen table, talking and smoking. And as she listened, she cleaned off the counter and straightened things up, paying attention and finding ways to organize the scraps of adult information while wiping up the rings of water on the surface, brushing up the crumbs, aligning the sponge in its dish next to the sink.

Carin's bedroom was the biggest room in her family's house, and it was furnished with a round table, two bar chairs, shelves full of art supplies. But she was happier in the kitchen, and to this day she loves housecleaning products. Perhaps it is because the little stacks of sponges, colored rags, jars of soap represent some idea, some coalition of things, ideas, order, attention. "I love cleaning supplies," she has told me more than once.

She is a gifted artist and has spent much of her professional life designing record albums, posters, book jackets, embroidered textiles. I'm as good a feminist as anyone and know it is foolish to think that tidying up has much to do with why she became an acclaimed designer. Yet at the same time I feel certain that her considerations of order and invention, her attentiveness to repetition and discipline, the manner in which she aligns images, letters, impressions to evoke small vignettes of human meaning, and her impulse to make the world a place you want to inhabit, which is to say, someplace deeply desirable, all carry some memory of putting things to right on that kitchen counter.

Housework II

I am folding the laundry and for no good reason the image of a river in the south of Mexico enters my mind. I am washing the dishes and am suddenly thinking of a turquoise iceberg I once saw in Iceland. Making the bed last week, I found myself thinking of my mother paying bills at her Chinese desk. It is a mystery to me why any of these things came into my mind when they did.

It turns out there is a name for such experiences: involuntary semantic memories or, in more popular jargon, mind pops. These describe the random imagery and thoughts that float into one's mind when one is occupied by dull routine tasks. I know little about the workings of the brain, neurology, or experimental psychology, but I know something about housework. Which means I know that it is exactly when one is doing tedious, repetitive things that the mind is free to fasten itself elsewhere, to unexpected memories and experiences all but forgotten.

Which is why it amazes me to hear people say they find housework dull. A snippet of a song, the expression on my son's face the summer afternoon he learned to swim, the sound of a foghorn in San Francisco. I don't know how any of these impressions are organized and stored in the archives of human memory, but it remains a marvel to me that all it takes is rinsing a glass or folding a dish towel to summon them up.

Bric-a-Brac

I read recently about a literary argument between two poets that took place in Key West in February 1940. Wallace Stevens said to Robert Frost, "Your trouble, Robert, is that you write poems about subjects." And Frost replied, "Your trouble, Wallace, is that your poems are about bric-a-brac."

Something about this exchange makes me incredibly happy. As though they are one of those cranky couples who have divided up the domestic chores, with one of them arranging what is outside the house, the other looking after what is inside. You look after the stone walls and the birches, and I'll attend to the coffee, the Seville oranges, the sunny chair, and the rug. They thought about stuff and then they fought about it. It is assumed that Stevens may have been drunk at the time, but no one is really sure, which pretty much makes it the same kind of vague conjecture people make when they are talking about other couples' fights.

The anecdote says something about the inanity of so many literary arguments. It also says something about the nutty possibilities of spring break for poets. But what it also suggests is that poetry and home design seem to exist in

parallel universes. They both consider arrangements
of space, color, texture, time of day, how the air feels, how
landscape and structure can meet, how light falls into
a room, how human beings can inhabit a space, how interior
and exterior space can converge—whatever, you get
my point.

Maybe the only real difference is that you have a
pretty clear idea what one is about and not the other. I know
what some things are for, like a chair or a rug or a stone wall.
I haven't a clue what poetry is for, though I think most of
us benefit from reading it from time to time. Although
I went to college in Vermont not far from where Frost once
lived, it was, weirdly enough, Stevens I remember reading
then. As ridiculous as it sounds, it was a time when you
could get stoned and talk about the word "innuendo"
for hours at a time. And then that phrase of his, "celestial
ennui." When you are eighteen and in college, you can
go on for months imagining how it is possible to attach
those two words to nearly every facet of your life. And actually, when I think about that now, that's about as close
as I've come to knowing what poetry is for.

It's been a while since I've given celestial ennui much
thought. But I've certainly been wondering lately how to tell
the difference between a subject and bric-a-brac. Or if there
even happens to be a difference. Because I suspect if this is

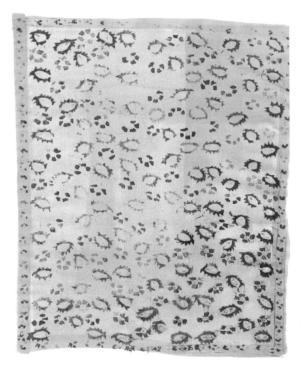

going to be resolved, it's not going to be by a couple
of poets arguing in Key West, but by a woman trying to
straighten out her house.

I am just such a woman, and here is what I can tell
you. It's not that these things are interchangeable, but
more that we often mistake one for the other. The things
you think are the knickknacks—your father's gold pen, your
mother's silk scarf, the row of shells on your window sill,
the blue ceramic teapot you bought in Rye—these are
subjects. Regardless of what they are saying in Key West,
I can promise you that.

Everything else is bric-a-brac. Your ideas of comfort
or what makes a room beautiful or your thoughts about
safety or privacy—the paint on all these will chip, their
edges fray, they'll get scuffed up and knocked over by some
guest, and then be forgotten. These are the miscellaneous
curios that will matter least. If you don't believe me, then
at the very least, when you are straightening up your living
room or dusting a shelf, you could do worse than to
treat bric-a-brac as a subject and a subject as nothing
more than a piece of bric-a-brac.

Museum

Last fall, my husband and I found a plague of black flies in our house. As with previous unexpected infestations— ladybugs, ants, stinkbugs—that we occasionally experience in our rural neighborhood, we searched out every available strategy. We put up a series of sticky traps on the windows, strips of clear pheromone-infused adhesive tape that the insects stuck to the instant they landed on them. The dozens of black flies that subsequently arranged themselves for the final time on the glass panes had a kind of improvised elegance, a miniature choreography of fatality that you wouldn't be surprised to find behind a frame at MoMA. And twirling merrily down from our shelves and ceilings were molasses-colored glue paper catchers, festive little streamers that were powerful exercises in nostalgia, urging me to revisit the old country kitchens and barns I remembered from my childhood.

On the mantle was a colorful hexagonal cylinder that my husband picked up at the hardware store. Twelve inches tall, its adhesive surface was patterned in turquoise and chartreuse spots and squiggles that were both random and repetitive. Its bright graphics were meant to attract the flies, but with a whimsical ambiguity that juxtaposed a sense of play with poison, it also had a level of philosophical content that evoked the work of the Italian designer Alessandro Mendini had he gone into pest removal. Then there were the flytraps left by the guy from Orkin; small folding white cardboard boxes with crisp red lettering and black diagramming outlining the details of their use, they had an industrial styling that conveyed a more modern sensibility. And a flyswatter with a vibrant, violet-hued mesh pad induced us into the requisite interactive relationship.

Living for that week in our little improvised art installation, I realized I still don't have a clue whether art imitates life or life imitates art. The question matters less, I think, than the knowledge and genuine comfort that can be derived in finding the vast and extravagant sensorium—the light, texture, aroma, color, graphics—the whole range of strategies available to us when we are trying to get rid of those things we don't want.

The Mighty Room

I came across a story in the *New York Times* last spring
called "Where the Spirit Moves You." It was about how
you could go to the Emily Dickinson homestead in Amherst,
Massachusetts, and for a few hundred dollars spend time
alone in the poet's room. And how the flowered wallpaper
and white dress and little wooden desk might become props
for your imagination. The article so amazed me that I went
to the museum's website, and sure enough, the program
called "Studio Sessions" invited visitors to have a "sweet
hour" of their own in the poet's bedroom.

The promotional copy quotes her poem: "Sweet
hours have perished here; / This is a mighty room; / Within
its precincts hopes have played,— / Now shadows in the
tomb." And then the copy invites visitors to spend their
own time in the poet's creative space where "she penned
her startling poetry" and how they will find "solace and
inspiration" there for their "own artistic output." And how
they can "let this quiet experience jumpstart your next
creative journey." Visitors must provide identification, are
only allowed to use pencils, and, speaking of startling

things, the bedroom door must be kept open at all times. So much for solitude.

I'm sympathetic to museums having to raise revenue. I once willingly spent thirty dollars to take my kids to Family Day at the Shaker Museum. Right? From a sect that prohibited procreation and didn't allow parents to raise their own children. But the idea of renting out time in Emily Dickinson's bedroom for a little creative time of your own may reflect some basic confusion about the poems, about solitude, in the same way Family Day at the Shaker Museum subverts that sect's beliefs about utopian living.

I try to imagine what the poet might have had to say about her readers spending hundreds of dollars to be alone in her room and the coy marketing suggestion that inhabiting the space of her poems is only the first step in the pricier project of inhabiting her bedroom. I'm not sure I know much about jumpstarting the human imagination, but I'm pretty sure I have this one thing right. You can do it in your own room. Or in your grandmother's kitchen, the closet under the stairs, your brother's coveted bedroom, the glassed-in room next to the porch, the messy garage full of tools, the forbidden room at the top of the stairs. These rooms hold their own sense of time, have their own presence and history. They are all full of stuff that may or may not furnish your life. Your ideas about interior and exterior space, and maybe even interior and exterior self, came from such rooms. Along with your ideas about the meaning of solitude, the accessories for privacy, how we share space with one another, the history of places, how the creative process takes root, and so on.

Whatever you happen to think about the engagement between the animate and inanimate worlds probably started in the rooms you lived in yourself. And whatever ideas you may have about how we conspire with the material world to live complete lives came from these rooms. You don't need the green velvet curtains or the antique floorboards or the little bed that the poet slept in. You don't need the little wooden desk or her white dress. You can just sit in the room and decide for yourself whether you would like the door to be open or closed. If it's the precincts of hope or the perishing of sweet hours you are after, any room of your own will work just as well.

The Door

It's not that I have any argument with the imperative of graciousness. Like most people, I value the ability with which we welcome people into our homes and the warmth we like to convey to them. Arrival has its own habits and decor, little welcome mats and a place to hang your coat.

But it occurs to me that skill in getting guests to go may be just as important. A woman I know was faced with just such a dilemma. Her houseguests, who had overstayed a short visit by two, then three days, exhibited no sign of leaving. They were indifferent to the hints of the hosts, impervious to the demands they were making on her own time and work. Finally, in frustration, the woman came up with an expedient gesture. After dinner one night she collected the plates, put them on the floor, allowed the dogs to lick them clean, then stacked them up and put them straight back into the cabinet. The guests looked on, appalled, then left before the next meal.

This story is nowhere near as revolting as it sounds. Rather, what it suggests is that departure has its own rituals and decor, its own scenery and accessories. Along with the idea that hospitality sometimes requires solitude and that the door out is every bit as important as the door in. That, as elsewhere in life, skill, imagination, and intelligence can be applied not just in letting people in, but in finding a way for them to go out.

Landscapes

My friend Brooke is easily described as an outdoor person. She is drawn to untended landscapes and has been known to ride ponies across Iceland's lava fields, bicycle across the Dutch floodplains, hike across the English Lake District. But the thing is, she cannot abide reading about the natural world. She teaches literature to college students and much prefers to read Charles Dickens, George Eliot, Anthony Trollope, Oscar Wilde, stories of urban street life, drawing room conversations, accounts of social manners, and all varieties of other interior narratives.

I try to imagine the opposite: a woman who owns nothing but cocktail dresses and is thrilled most by museum openings, dinner parties, literary theory, and the history of architecture, but who reads nothing save essays by Robert Macfarlane about all the words that may exist for the pebbles on the Scottish moors, John Wesley Powell's accounts of the unforeseen eddies and rapids in the Colorado River, Aldo Leopold's contemplation of why he favors the white pine over the red birch, and his thoughts on how there is "skill in the exercise of bias." I wonder if such a woman exists.

I also wonder whether the literary imagination and the material world have anything to do with each other. Maybe they do and maybe they don't. But what I wonder most is whether it is the contrary nature of human behavior or simply our own native skill in the exercise of bias that enables us to parcel out the real estate of our sensibilities to such distant and different countries.

Paint Job

As we were raising our two sons, my husband and I did something many families do. As the boys were growing up, we documented their increasing height with marks on the kitchen door frame, little pencil scratches indicating their growth from three to four to five feet tall, and more. But at some point well into this practice, as these scribbles had laddered up the blue doorframe, we needed to have the kitchen repainted.

Because we wanted to preserve this little improvisational record of our sons' lives, we gave the painter clear directives to leave the frame untouched. We came home at the end of the afternoon after the kitchen had been painted and found he had forgotten our instructions. The room gleamed with the coat of fresh paint, and the record of measurements on the door frame had been obliterated entirely. The painter was practically weeping with remorse. He did not know what he was doing, he told us. He had simply forgotten, realizing his mistake only later. He was terribly, terribly sorry. He knew there was no way he could correct his error or make it up to us. "It's okay," we told him. We understood how such things can happen.

Many months later, I happened to learn from a neighbor that the painter had lost his own son years earlier at a young age in a freak farm accident. He had managed to find some way to live with this loss, to go on, but every year on the boy's birthday, he took the day off and got blind drunk. I wonder about the afternoon he spent painting our kitchen. I doubt that he was consciously aware of what he was doing as he rolled the blue paint evenly over all those dates of our sons' ongoing lives. Yet in asking him to honor these little measurements, I thought about how likely it was that we had asked him to do something difficult, if not unbearable. And about how we have such little knowledge of the lives of others and how terribly and impossibly wrong even our smallest expectations of them can often be.

Proxy

The email from the office in the town hall stated it simply: the following day, the utility company would be floating a four-foot diameter orange balloon above the woods where a proposed cell tower was to be built. One hundred and fifty feet above the ground and attached to a tether line, the balloon was to signal the location and height of the proposed structure, thus allowing residents to consider its impact on the landscape and viewshed.

I looked for the balloon the following morning. I couldn't see it from the driveway, nor as I drove down the road, nor from the gas station down at the corner. When I headed up the hill a mile or so, it appeared briefly at the crest of the hill, hovering gently above the hickories, ash, and maples. It was nothing to object to, and I drove home.

The cell tower may or may not be built on this wooded hillside. But what lingers with greater certainty in my imagination is the idea of the balloon and its function as a cheerful little placeholder for what's to come. And suddenly it is easy to imagine these orange balloons floating everywhere. Sometimes they are visible and sometimes not, but they are there—in the kitchen, above the garden, on the side porch, bright souvenirs from a party thrown for all those things, people, events, words we cannot yet even dream of.

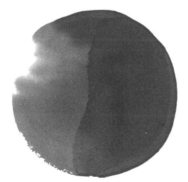

Trees

Some friends of mine recently made a cross-country road trip. Along the way, they stopped to visit a boyhood home of Abraham Lincoln. Outside of the cabin were several saplings. My friends were told as an aside by the guide that these small trees were dug up and replaced every few years so that the plantings around the little house remained botanically consistent with the image of a young boy growing into manhood.

The more I think about this, the more I find that it is one of those absurd facts that make all the sense in the world. Really, it is just an extreme version of what so many of us do, which is to try and see things in the natural world that reflect something true about who we are.

But I remain curious about those discarded saplings. Are they carefully dug up and replanted elsewhere in local streets and parks? Are they sold as quasi-historical trees? Are they cut down and shredded for mulch? Because where and how *they* end up may be what says the most about how we look to the natural world as a place—or more precisely, a landscape for dislocation—that reflects human impulse and incident.

Furniture

A friend of mine came to dinner the other night. She
is a good friend and is in and out of my house fairly
frequently. This time she admired a walnut cabinet in the
living room, appreciating the way the new piece of furniture fit the room. I told her it had been there for the last
five years. There is a name for this, "change blindness,"
a phenomenon that prevents us from seeing what is right
in front of our eyes only because it is not what we expect
and not what we have seen before. Our memory encodes
the familiar at the expense of what is actually there.

I don't know that there has been any research on this,
but I suspect it's a condition that occurs most often on
home territory. Sometimes it is about the walnut cabinet,
the oak end table by the sofa, or the metal spice rack over
the stove, but more often it's not about the decor, but
about human behavior. It is in our nature to form abiding
attachments to the familiar, and it is why so many families
argue at the Fourth of July picnic or fall into mayhem at
the Thanksgiving table: it is almost impossible for family

members to recognize change in one another although it is there right before them. We are all likely to treat people close to us the way we treated them two years ago, or five or ten. Which is to say, like furniture.

Music

When I was in elementary school, my parents had the idea that I should learn to play the piano. To that end, they installed a grand piano that had belonged to my grandmother in a small room in the back of the barn. Because the room was not heated in the winter, they also put a small electric heater in the room, and I would go out there on weekday afternoons to practice.

Looking back on this, I know it is inconceivable that it ever happened. It would have been impossible to move a grand piano through the series of small doors leading to that little room in the back of the barn. Doors and walls would have had to have been removed, and this never happened either. But I am just as sure it was not an upright piano because I remember exactly how the light falling through the window illuminated the thin blanket of dust covering the vast lid of the grand piano. I had no musical ear, my fingers were always cold, the dust in the back room made me sneeze, and even an exercise so simple as practicing the scales produced a sound that was almost impossible to identify. So maybe, I think, it was the gargantuan task of trying to learn to play this piano that caused me to so magnify its size; and that occasioned me to translate my monumental efforts into a monumental instrument.

I know that places exist in memory almost entirely differently than they exist in the material world. And that the houses in our recall are furnished not only with pianos that can move through walls, but floorboards that shift, light that adjusts magically, windows that alter their position. I am certain that the stone path leading to our front door in the house we live in today is original to the old farmhouse, but my husband swears to laying down the stones himself, placing them just so. Just as the keys of the piano have come to reflect a fantasia of octaves, the arrangement of stones manages to reflect different sequences of conviction. Perhaps I associate the path with some kind of domestic history or legacy that matters to me, while in my husband's mind it is connected with the way he laid out our own route to the house. What seems certain either way is that the tenacity of the material world is nothing when it comes up against the tenacity of human memory.

Step

The old farmhouse my family lives in was added onto incrementally, with rooms added over the last two centuries. For this reason, the kitchen that was built at one end of the house required a ten-inch step up from the dining room next to it.

When the boys were six, we got a husky puppy who was promptly named Wolfie, and Wolfie found this step troublesome. It was not just the shift in elevation, but the change in flooring material from the blue linoleum tiles of the kitchen to the chestnut boards of the dining room that freaked him out. The change in space, material, color, texture—it was all too much for him, and no manner of cajoling or treats could convince the pup to leave the kitchen. Even if one of the boys carried him tenderly out of the kitchen and rewarded the successful transit with biscuits, Wolfie trotted back to the kitchen at the earliest opportunity. We finally gave into this, put his little bed in the kitchen, and let him claim that space as his own, figuring he would eventually find his own way into the rest of the house.

This never happened. Weeks after Wolfie's arrival into our family, our vet detected a slight involuntary twitching of

Wolfie's head, a signal of a neurological disorder. The dog's attachment to the kitchen was the least of his troubles. While he often gazed at us with quizzical eyes, he was short on affection, growling at visitors, and most content when he was curled up alone. Seizures came next, and his short life ended when he was less than two years old, with a grand mal fit from which he never recovered.

We got the puppy for all the usual reasons: faith, love, companionship, the abiding trust one finds in canine eyes, lessons in the responsibility of care and its rewards that a family pet offers. Our boys experienced little of this with the disturbed dog often found cowering at the forbidding drop of the kitchen step. If there were lessons at all, they had more to do with estrangement, distance, and how human care can sometimes be inadequate to the needs of those around us. But still, I am certain my sons' experience had value. Because surely they learned something then about how affection is not always reciprocal and how it is possible to love and not be loved in return.

Tarps

Of course we use different kinds of language to talk about different facets of our lives. Some parts of human experience ask for reflective contemplation while others demand more decisive clinical prose; we talk to our closest friends in a different way than we talk to our doctors. Yet I wonder sometimes if these categories of jargon could be more porous. And if we might apply the expressive language that is so often used for rooms and furniture and gardens to some of the more prosaic materials that are essential to the way we live. For example: the shining rectangle of cobalt over my head after the March storm. Nothing but an iridescent lapis membrane, it managed to repel the freezing rain and withstand the wind, still catching the afternoon light, and by dusk, the wrapping evoked an arrangement by Christo, creating its own puzzles of surface and form, enigmas of the hidden and exposed, all the while responding to the uncertainties of the early spring skies. I am speaking, of course, about roof tarps. If the way we use words reflects where and how we find beauty in ordinary things, it occurs to me that in a time of hurricanes, tornados, erosion, mudslides, floods, lava flow, and other circumstances of extreme weather, it would be helpful for us to find a descriptive and evocative language for tarps that is similar to the language we use for mid-century lighting fixtures or heirloom Chippendale or French wallpaper.

Theater

I recently heard about an experimental British theater company that has produced thirty-six of the Bard's plays using everyday objects to represent the characters. In "Tabletop Shakespeare," a spool of thread, a beer bottle, and a pitcher all become players, their drama narrated over the landscape of a kitchen table. Henry V is a candlestick; Macbeth, a jar of linseed oil; a messenger is represented by a water bottle, a servant by a spoon.

In the YouTube clip I watched, there *was* something mesmerizing in watching Claudius as a can of flea powder and Gertrude as a silver pot as they tried to reason with the salt and pepper shakers, Rosencrantz and Guildenstern. And already I'm looking at the objects resting on the shelf above my kitchen sink—an old teacup, some coins, a glass bottle, a ceramic plum, a Dutch ceramic bowl glazed with a garland of blue flowers. I could give them all names! Ophelia, Lysander, King Richard! It takes nothing for us to give voices to things, to invest character and meaning into inanimate objects.

I'm not quite sure why such a ridiculous device works so well. Maybe it has to do with how we *know* that small things can become large and large things can become small. Or that there is a thin line between what is ordinary and what is extraordinary. Or that the way things are arranged and rearranged in a domestic space can reveal something true. Or that it takes no effort at all for us to give voices to things, to invest character and meaning into inanimate objects. Or perhaps it just has to do with the fact that language can surpass the truth of what we see in front of our eyes. And that the right words will make us believe anything.

The Turf Hut

"Adorable" is not an adjective you find yourself using very often in Iceland, where the landscape tends toward glacial flow, heart-stopping waterfalls, vast and ashen volcanic plains. But it was exactly the word that came to mind the day my friends and I visited the turf houses. We couldn't help but be charmed by the little grassy roofs, wee gables framed by whiskery weeds, the azure blue walls, the handsewn coverlets. These little houses are not so much sited in the landscape as snuggled. They really are. The rooms in this particular complex are labyrinthine, tiny bedrooms and sitting rooms leading one to another; we sent a photo of one of these huts to a friend who has a house in East Hampton. She is an interior designer and texted back, "Must have turf house."

She is a kind, smart, funny woman and is often given to such humor. Still, it is not hard to imagine these cozy little sod houses being the next thing everyone does in the name of sustainability on their beach properties. Or to envision all these little eco-shacks sprouting up on the back lawns of the gleaming glass palaces of eastern Long Island as the living quarters for home chefs, personal trainers, and life coaches. It could happen.

Here is the thing about turf houses: If you had, in fact, lived in one of these a century or so ago you would, over the course of a winter, have found it a place of infestation—dark, damp, full of stagnant air. Your children's hair would be crawling with lice. The foul stench from the animals and humans would be unbearable, but not nearly as awful as the insects and worms crawling out of the walls that would leave you with open sores and bloody lesions all over your skin.

I'm not a complete idiot. I know that if the idea of turf houses gets reinvented for the twenty-first century, it will be with new composite materials, ventilation, solar illumination, and so on. But the minute I write this I think, wait, I may even be wrong here. Because you know as well as I do that it is equally possible, especially now that you can buy such a thing as antibacterial interior wall paint, that it's not going to be long before someone will be telling you the insects and worms crawling out of the walls is something to be desired, good for your chi or good for your immune system, or good for god knows what else. The infertility and birth defects in mice exposed to such paint is already a matter of record. As far as I can tell, it's only a matter of time before the insects and worms become the next thing.

I am constantly amazed by what people believe. And I marvel at the way, in a landscape of tectonic plates that appear to have crashed into each other just about yesterday, a place where glaciers unfurl themselves right down to the road you are driving on and where meadows of black lava stretch as far as you can see, that we are moved to find things that could best be described as "cute." But honestly, what astonishes me most is our inability to see misery when it is staring us in the face because we think we could be made happy by this room, or that.

Tedium

When I was in college in the seventies, I worked for a short time at an insurance company. The school gave students two months off in the winter to work—theoretically as interns in their chosen fields, but probably, we suspected, to save the cost of heating the dorms. In any event, for those two months I moved to Hartford, Connecticut, not because I wanted a job in the insurance industry, but because I was dating a boy who lived in Hartford.

I got the job at the Aetna headquarters through Kelly Girl Service, the postwar employment company that found temporary staff positions for low-level office workers. So for those two months I was a file clerk. This was before the time of electronic records, so each morning I was given hundreds of folders of client paperwork that had been used by the adjustors the previous day or week, and I filed these alphabetically in the cabinets where they belonged. It was dull, monotonous, repetitive work. I remember the long alleys of beige cabinets, the expansive glass windows that looked out across the dusty rooftops of the city to the pale winter sky beyond. As a temporary worker I was anonymous, all but nameless. In an ironic twist, the two months I spent reading the names of policy holders and determining the exact location of where the facts of their lives belonged in the vast customer catalogue were a time when my own identity seemed insignificant.

I knew the poet Wallace Stevens had also worked at a Hartford insurance company, but I had no idea at all how he thought his literary life and business life might, or might not, coalesce. But those weeks among the file cabinets allowed me to imagine I was on some periphery of his experience. I knew I was just a college kid with a temporary gig, while he was a lawyer and vice president of the company he worked for. Still, the businessman in the gray suit with the executive job spent much of his life considering insurance claims in a world that was remote from the bohemian extravaganzas so common to those years. During that time, he wrote some of the most shining poems of the twentieth century. And I began to consider those ways in which order and routine can abet the human imagination. And how tedium and incandescence can be unexpectedly strong partners.

I was raised on the belief that it is the work of writers rather than their lives that should hold our interest. And I believe that today. But there is something, too, in sidling up to the life of another—or perhaps it is simply the *illusion* of sidling up to another life—that can be illuminating. Or maybe it's some question of spatial proximity, real or imagined.

We can come to know people through their words and actions, but still, there is something about places, rooms that can alert us to some intrinsic quality in the lives of others in the way that nothing else can. And I know that my appreciation for Stevens's work resides, just a bit, in my two months at Aetna and in those bland corridors that must have been known to him as well.

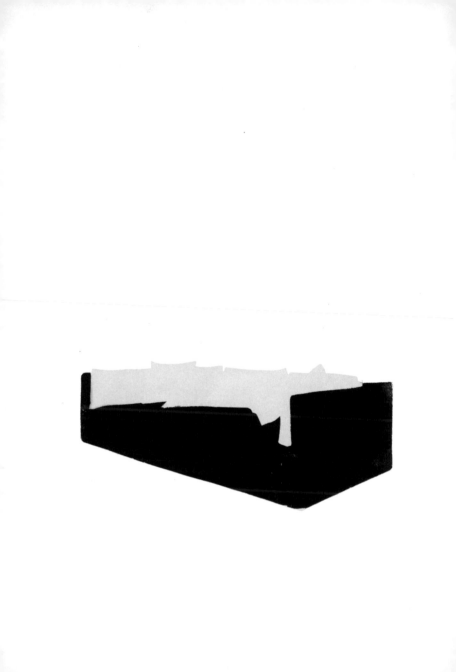

Sofa

From the beginning, the blue sofa was too large for the room. A monstrosity upholstered in crushed velvet, it had been left by a previous tenant in an apartment that was far too small for its huge cushions and its massive arms. I tried to think of the color as a deep Mediterranean blue, but in fact it was an ordinary dark navy. It seemed to consume the space, and somewhere in the first few weeks I lived there its monumental presence and immense weight came to represent all those other troubles that seem to persist.

I couldn't move the thing myself, so I asked the Salvation Army to come and take the sofa away. The man I spoke with gave me a seven-hour window of time during which the moving truck would come for it, and I agreed to be there for every minute of that time. But when I arrived home that afternoon to wait, the truck had come and gone twenty minutes earlier than the time stated. A few days later, a friend of mine told me he would take it away but he had to find someone to help him, and he didn't know how long that would take. The sofa continued to squat there with all its acquired malevolence. That the inanimate world has a tenacity all its own was not news to me.

And then one afternoon several weeks later, I walked into the apartment. In the first few seconds, I knew that something essential had happened, but I didn't know what. The air in the room had changed. And then I realized: My friend had found someone to help and had let himself in. The sofa was gone. Where it had been were only a few scratches on the floor, some dust—a few spectral vestiges of its vast presence. Suddenly, it was a memory.

And I remembered how I had once been on West 25th Street in Manhattan when a forty-ton piece of sculpture by Richard Serra was being moved out of a gallery. A crane was lifting the gigantic hunk of elliptical steel. People had gathered on the sidewalk to watch. "It's like going to the moon," said a man standing beside me. And I thought also of the artist Michael Heizer, who made arrangements to have a two-story rock weighing 340 tons trucked 110 miles from the desert in Riverside, California, to a museum in Los Angeles. The truck had 176 wheels and a bed that was 300 feet long and it traveled that distance between five and eight miles an hour for eleven nights.

I realized that in some funny way, accommodating a massive shift in the weight of things seems to happen both instantaneously and lasts over a long period of time.

I thought there must be some psychological corollary and I asked a friend of mine who is a therapist if there is a word for this. "You mean breakthrough," she said.

And I realized, too, this is how things so often exit our lives. We beg for them to be gone, have fantasies of that empty space and how we will put it to use. And then when it finally happens, neither the eye nor brain can quite fathom the absence. It takes a moment or two to register the empty space. And I can't say now which is more important, acquiring things or getting rid of them. I know that comfort and how we furnish a room has something to do with how objects come into our lives. But I am certain that the way things leave us matters just as much.

The Stove

One of my first jobs when I graduated from college was at a design magazine. Such publications were called shelter magazines, and the stories often involved slipcovers and curtains, floor treatments and layouts. They were written to get readers to buy new accessories for their homes. But in this case, the editor, a visionary woman named Susan Szenasy, had a strong interest in design history. In February 1980, she ran a cover with a picture of a Chinese mud stove in a peasant house. The United States and China had recently reestablished trade relations, and US companies—and journalists—were taking a new interest in Chinese culture.

While the picture of the kitchen spoke to a new era in global commerce, the image did not appeal much to the magazine's advertisers. But it redefined design for me. It was a watershed moment, the first time design became something interesting to me, something larger than what I had supposed. I began to understand design as a kind of social and cultural phenomenon; how the shape of the physical world, whether it is a bracelet or a building, both reflects and influences who we are. The more I read and studied, the more I found this to be so. And so this intersection of objects and material culture began to engage me. The little picture of the stove changed the direction of my thinking.

Four decades later, I happened to be reading the newspaper one morning, and there was an obituary of an environmental scientist. His groundbreaking work in global health had grown during the many years he had spent researching the toxic effects of the mud and clay cooking stoves used by some forty percent of the world's population— and especially by those in emerging nations. His research exposed how such cookstoves, using fuels derived from firewood, charcoal, or cow dung could cause pollution, disease, early death. "We've realized that pollution may start in the kitchen, but it doesn't stay there," he was quoted as saying in the article.

And so I stood corrected. What I had viewed once as an example of native tradition and handcrafted skill that could enrich the thinking of people living in developed countries was, in fact, an agent of toxicity. This amazed me. Not the fact that the story that had so changed my thinking was the wrong story, but rather the idea that it is possible that even those stories that change the course of your life can later be rewritten completely.

Wallpaper

I'm flipping through a book of wallpaper patterns when
I come across a document of disappeared species. The
collection is called "The Museum of Extinct Animals," and
it depicts a jungle of vanished birds, animals, fish, insects.
The phantasmagoric parade of umbrella squid, blushing
sloths, bearded leopards, flying coral fish, dwarf rhino,
blooming sea dragons has been taken from old photographs,
botanical drawings, and etchings, all of which, the promotional copy says, are "museum quality." The lavish composition is also a convergence of beauty, apprehension, disquiet.
Textured, lush, a gorgeous extravaganza of extinction—
it'll be a favorite on Instagram in no time.

But this is, I know, in the tradition of wallpaper. Funerals
and wars have also been popular motifs. I read somewhere
that Jackie Kennedy papered the White House with panels
depicting scenes from the American Revolution. Maybe
panoramas of trauma are a niche market. Maybe there is
something here about how we commemorate absence.
And I look at the velvety fur of the blushing sloth, the shim-
mering blue beak of the dodo, the sapphire eye of a plaid

zebra. It is easy to disparage this pricey wallpaper and its dazzling menagerie of disappearance, but all the same it does something real. And though it might not quite be museum quality, I still say it is historically correct in that it lays out precisely this compulsion we so often have to fashion something decorative out of anxiety, damage, and loss.

Placement

A man I know loves loading the dishwasher. He treats it as a superlative skill. Which in his case, it is. But the thing is, he's an actor. This is a little locus of order for him, and when he is at work in the kitchen, he will make certain the cups and bowls and mugs nestle into each other against the prongs of the upper rack, readjusting the wine glass and the salad plate on the lower one, removing the knife with the wood handle that does not belong there. He builds the equivalent of a little nest every evening, sliding and fitting all the pieces of the puzzle together, before the action starts: flashing lights, the sound of rushing water, the clouds of steam and air!

When I first saw him do this, it made me think of the washer as a little theater, and how his sense of absolute placement must have come from being an actor and understanding staging and how people learn to situate themselves—in space, with things. But then I wondered if it was the opposite. Maybe he became an actor because he learned the art of placement and where things belong when he was cleaning up, loading the dishwasher.

It's a little manic, this kind of thinking, the sort of frantic conjecture that does nothing but loop around on itself. I know that. Just as I know this actor learned his craft by paying attention, having a sensitivity to voice, to sound, to the rhythm of language, to the behavior of those around him, to the way people arrange themselves in space, to the way people see and speak and move through the world, with grace or without. But all the same that dishwasher lingers in my mind, reminding me that it is entirely possible for people to find ways to practice what they know and love in small, common places that are worlds away from where they do their best work.

The Cracked Tile

It doesn't necessarily have anything to do with ownership.
It just has to do with living someplace. Because as soon as
you do, you realize how many things remain unfinished. The
door frame that needs paint. The window that doesn't quite
shut. A light fixture that needs to be rewired. These things that
never quite get done and are never forgotten—I learned
recently of a name for this, the "Zeigarnik effect."

The term comes from the psychologist who researched
the way in which a waiter in a café spent the greatest time and
attention on those customers who had not yet paid their bills.
How obvious, you must be thinking, of course, of course. But
when you look this up in Wikipedia, you will also encounter
the phrase "advantage of recollection," which is about the way
we remember things best when they have been interrupted
and how students who take breaks in their studies will remember what they have been studying more clearly than those
students who do not take a break.

I was a waitress once in college, so all this makes sense
to me. I think back to that time and try to remember what
I remembered. But it just turns out to be a silly Russian doll

exercise of human recall. Sometimes I remembered customers, but I am not sure it had to do with whether they had paid their bills.

And now when I look at the dripping pipe beneath the kitchen sink or the pane of glass that needs to be reglazed, I no longer even consider repairing these things, but wonder instead if it is an advantage or disadvantage of recollection that whether it is a cracked tile on the kitchen floor or a letter half written or a conversation in a bar on a June evening, those things we remember most clearly are so often those that remain interrupted, incomplete, undone.

Air

The *New York Times* reported recently that South Koreans believe electric fans can kill you. The frigid air they generate is thought to cause hypothermia and possibly even organ failure. Or they can be just as likely to suck out all the oxygen in the air, inducing suffocation. Or possibly, oxygen molecules can be converted into carbon dioxide by such fans. While none of these is on record as ever actually happening, such worries persist and fan deaths are reported regularly in the Korean news media, even despite speculation the entire thing was dreamed up by a previous government regime that had hopes of reducing the electric use of its population. I find it hard to fathom any of this. During the summer months I rely on the white fan in the kitchen with its curved white blades and their gay, competent rotations. A vertical unit in the study is equipped with multiple adjustments and lights that indicate speed, time, direction, and in the bedroom a standing fan with four different breeze settings can be counted on to draw in and circulate the cool evening air.

Animated, energetic, and lively, these appliances function something like a herd of obedient little household pets, blinking, humming, and whirring us into coolness. I think about how outlandish our fears are, especially at home, where the ideas we have about security and domestic comfort, our level of interest in consumer products, inexplicable cultural convictions, and the twists and turns of our own psyches can all converge to construct particularly weird anxieties. Then my mind wanders to all those things that *have* generated fear in my own household—the pack of American Spirit cigarettes I once saw peeking out from the pocket of a babysitter's denim jacket, my son's black rat snake that escaped its cage in the kitchen, a teenager who is suddenly as silent as a Trappist monk, familial discord at the dining room table, the sudden estrangements of spirit among stable adults who should know better, and all those times when a bad wind just blows through the whole house for no good reason—which makes me think the South Koreans may have it right after all.

Coins

Sitting on the windowsill above my desk is an 1826 Coronet Liberty copper penny. A man using a metal detector found it buried on the hill right outside the door. We had given him permission to search our land. He was a meteorologist by profession, a fact that made for an appealing symmetry; in his free time, he turned his gaze downward for artifacts buried in the ground. That year, the earth had not yet frozen in December. He told us that he would have preferred to do his detecting after there had been a day or two of rain "so that the grass can grow back green instead of brown," but in winter it didn't matter much.

Metal detectors produce an audio signal when they pass over metal, so he'd worn headphones that could discriminate between silver, brass, and copper buried up to twelve . inches beneath the surface. Then he used a hand trowel or screwdriver rather than a pickaxe or shovel to dig holes that he promised us would be no wider than his hand. After he'd dug up whatever he'd found, he folded the dirt and grass back down over the exposed patch so you'd never know he'd been there. He'd try to leave the area the way he found it, he told us.

Our house was built in 1792 so it's no surprise that all kinds of historic artifacts turned up. We are a burying species as well as a building species, the writer Robert Macfarlane has observed, and he uses the term "undersight" to describe the way we might call these things into view. And it was true that place and time coincide on our grassy hill. A few afternoons later, the man showed us what he'd found: miscellaneous coins, among them two "Rosies" that turned out to be old Roosevelt dimes, an early Indian Head penny, and a 1780s copper coin minted during the time this land was part of Connecticut instead of New York. A tiny hole had been punched into it so that it could be threaded on a string and worn. There was also an old USPS key, a nineteenth-century brass watch winder, a button from the 1820s with a steam locomotive carved onto its surface, a pockmarked iron shovel, a women's compact, a small toy airplane, some nails, an octagonal cufflink, and a belt buckle. None of these things were buried here for a reason; there was nothing votive or ceremonial about any of them. All the same, they recalled and even honored another time.

A couple of times, I had found myself running out to warn him about a spot he was working on. "Wait," I told him, "that's where the old oil tank was before it was dug up and taken apart. The ground there has already been turned up so you may not find anything." And there was a spot he was heading to where we had buried our dog, Wolfie. Had we interred him with his collar and tags? I couldn't remember. It amazed me that searching out these items, that is to say, our aptitude for undersight, is a matter of listening as well as seeing. What amazed me even more was that I knew anything at all about the archive of things that were buried here.

Signs

Some friends of mine came to dinner last week. As they arrived, they handed me a narrow white paper bag, inside of which was an expensive bottle of white balsamic vinegar. I was happy to have it, but the paper bag was what caught my eye. It was white with a logo in the center, a circle outlined in dark forest green, and inside the circle, an intertwined G and C, letters surrounded by the words "Williams-Sonoma Grande Cuisine."

I knew this logo well. I lived in San Francisco once, decades ago, when the company that came up with this brand was just starting out in a small store full of exotic and expensive kitchenware, shining toasters, and beautiful white French country tableware. My boyfriend and I lived in a small apartment. We weren't able to afford any of those things, yet somehow I had managed to have a little white canvas tote bag with the same logo from that store.

I used the tote bag a lot, but I remember it being most indispensable during that time I broke up with my boyfriend, suddenly and quickly one night. I stuffed some things in the bag—a blue shirt, a green sweater, a book, a cassette tape, a few other things—and I left the apartment. I didn't quite know where I was going and spent the next few weeks on the sofas and in the spare bedrooms of friends. Eventually I found a new place to live, got some furniture and kitchen things, but I remember those weeks, then months, as one of those times when nearly everything I did seemed like a colossal mistake.

And now, even all these years later, when I see that little green intertwined G and C on some bag or appliance, I don't recognize it as some little insignia of the good life. My reaction has nothing to do with elegant dinners or perfectly set tables with chic striped placemats. I do not think of gleaming pasta makers and blenders, Le Creuset pots, or virgin olive oils from Italy with lovely hand-drawn labels. Instead, I think of sleeplessness, hangovers, aspirin, loneliness, the fog in North Beach during a cold summer, the worry in my mother's voice on the telephone three thousand miles away in New York, and all manner of uncertainty of the worst order. By some weird fluke of circumstance, G & C was also the name of the bar on Green Street where I spent a lot of time in those days, so a beat-up pool table, deficient lighting, and streaked shot glasses are the accessories those initials evoke most clearly.

I understand about branding. I understand about that practice of arranging letters and signs and little shapes to

have them construct an entirely new meaning that has
to do with beauty or speed or efficiency or luxury, or whatever
else it happens to be. But what I don't understand at all is
why the people who make these logos and then apply them to
bags and appliances and household goods and clothes and
everything else are so certain we will attach that same meaning to them.

Because, of course, we don't. My kitchen now is a room
I love. The ash cabinets were built by my husband, the same
man I left that night in San Francisco all those years ago.
We have the imported olive oil now, and a blue Le Creuset
stew pot and a little Italian espresso maker. This room is
a place of sufficiency in every sense of the word. In an effusive
moment, I might even imagine it as Grande Cuisine. But even
today, when I happen to glance at the green circle and letters
on the white paper bag that the vinegar came in and that
is hanging on a doorknob in the kitchen now, what I think of
most is not having any of this at all.

Construction

The edge of the marsh is in a condition of botanical
havoc with a mess of toppled trees, a few shredded young
maples, and birch saplings tattered on the ground, the
brush and shrubbery around them torn to bits. What
remains of the trees are spears of exposed heartwood,
shaped by the beavers' incisions into jagged, abrupt points.
I know that the rodents often try to fell the trees they cut
in the direction of the water, but honestly, this looks like
a more slapdash operation.

And nothing about this quarter-acre of devastation
is static. Along with demolishing the trees, whose roots
will now fail to hold the bank together, the beavers have
been burrowing in, causing the ground to erode even
further. I wouldn't be surprised to see the contours of the
marsh reshaped entirely. The creek running through it
has already begun to flood into a small pool, contained at
one end by the palace of twigs, sticks, leaves, branches,
mud, and rock, and that pool widens by the day, the week.
But if the integrity of the bank has been degraded, the

construction out there is an imposing edifice. Engineered with only the most fragile parts, it is a sturdy reminder that even in habitats of the natural world, demolition and invention are natural, inevitable, and equal partners.

The Room

When my sister and I were kids, my family lived in Southeast Asia. In the summer of 1958, when I was five, we moved to the United States. We spent that first summer on Cape Cod, at our grandparents' shingled ranch house. In subsequent years, that house became a year-round residence. Additions were built, a master bedroom suite constructed, a deck added. But that summer, it was little more than a fifties ranch.

The room I remember most, where my sister and I spent the most time, was the living room. My mother had lovingly brought with us our carved Siamese desks, tiny bamboo chairs, a small teak table, but it was our grandfather's revolving chair that gave us the greatest comfort. Squat, square, upholstered in some synthetic fabric the color of dust, the chair was positioned on a fully rotational base, enabling its occupant to turn a full 360 degrees.

In retrospect, it was a feat of postwar engineering, a physical representation of the marvelous idea that the fifties might be a time when one's perspective on the world knew no limit. But for my sister and me such a chair was a carnival ride, and we spent hours spinning one another around and around. It was the ultimate in human engineered furniture. For kids who had just come halfway around the world, the spinning of the chair was a giddy relocation—one that we could handle, that made us happy, that thrilled us.

The room was also equipped with another staple of fifties design: a huge plate glass window. The view stretched from the intimate to the grand, from the patio and my grandfather's rose garden to the marsh of seagrass beyond, to the sliver of beach beyond that, and then to the bay where all manner of sailboats drifted by all day long. This was a picture window in every sense; even a kid knows that a view of the ocean is a view to infinite possibilities. Much later in my life, a designer told me—with respect to having a desk near a window—that it is healthy "to look at infinity." His statement took me back to that summer and my grandparents' plate glass window.

There were plenty of other things in that room— armchairs, a chinoiserie desk, big chunky glass ashtrays, stacks of magazines, and *Readers Digest* condensed books. But it is the chair and the window that I most remember. One of them could spin me around until I was dizzy. The other provided a view that was nearly endless. And I know now that whether it is furniture or something else completely, whatever offers such experiences are enough to furnish a room.

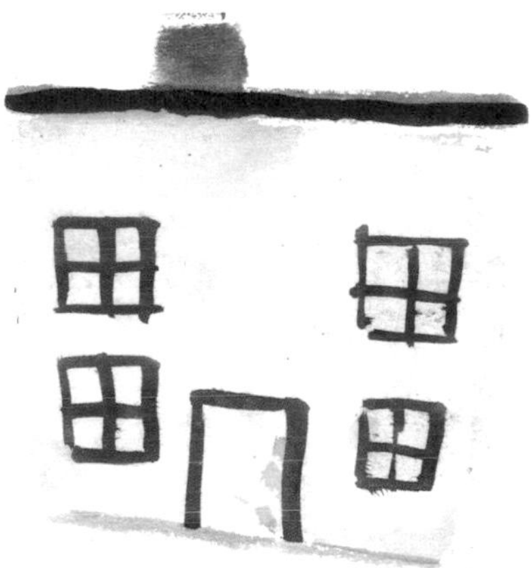

Peonies

It is June, and the garden's peony bushes are about to bloom. Which means that even before they open they have begun to droop and topple, their thin stems bending forward from the weight of the flower head. It may be the moisture or humidity in the air that makes the flowers so heavy that they begin their demise even as they reach full flower. Or maybe it is some botanical error intrinsic to this plant. I have no idea. But even their rich fuchsia color seems to add to their bulk. And although this has happened every spring for thirty-five years, it always surprises me, the inability of this plant to right itself, to correct its sense of load, mass, time.

Yet I find now that I welcome such miscalculations. It is not so different from seeing the sculpture by Christo floating on the Serpentine Lake in London's Hyde Park. Sixty-six feet tall and weighing six hundred tons, it was made of 7,506 stacked oil barrels attached to a steel structure. Still, it hovered on the surface of the water, a confusion of air and substance. Defying expectation, it contradicts our intuitive understanding about the physics and engineering of physical matter. And looking at the peonies now, I assume there is something to be learned from the unpredictable weights and measures of the material world.

Function

In our living room is an old fireplace that has been boarded
up and plastered over for the years we have lived in the
house. Below the mantel, toward the lower left of the panel
concealing the firebox is a small iron door, eight by ten
inches or so, set in a frame just slightly larger. The door has
a little latch, and words formed in raised letters that read
POUGHKEEPSIE IRON FOUNDRY, 1847. B. ARNOLD & SON.
Though it is covered with many layers of paint, the door and
its letters, little hinge, and latch all speak to precision, purpose, efficiency. The house was built in 1792 by the owner
of the local ironworks. We assume that this original fireplace
was blocked off, replaced by a wood-burning stove and
the little door, so clearly identified, served as a cleanout for
the soot in the flue just above it.

But that was more than a century and a half ago, and
the pointless little door on the nonfunctioning fireplace
is only one of many useless features of our old house. There
is also a door to the side porch that has never been opened,
as neither the porch nor the living room to which it leads
needs another entryway. And a crawlspace tucked into the

peak of the roof that is too small and cramped to get into or even to put anything in.

Once I thought it would be ingenious to find a use for all these outdated features. Things exist for a reason. Renovate the fireplace to get it burning, swing open the redundant door, store the boys' toys in the little crawlspace. That resolve has long since vanished. Instead, I have come to value these little pockets of dysfunction. Or not dysfunction, actually. Rather, I value them as remnants of function, a different thing entirely. It is easy to find pleasure in the tenacity of useless things. Utility, I know now, has its own rhythms and cycles, and a sense of purpose is as temporary in the material world as it is anyplace else.

Night Sky

I read recently of a mother and father in Mount Dora, Florida, who painted their house to resemble Van Gogh's *The Starry Night* so their adult, autistic son could find his way home. It was not difficult for their son to get lost in this city, and they felt that if he could just describe his house to strangers, those people would know the landmark building he was looking for and help him get home. There was a brief tussle with the city and a few neighbors, who felt the design did not conform to the local aesthetic or that it might distract drivers. But in the end, everyone agreed that the parents had the right to paint their house with the radiant night sky—its explosions of stars, its swirling meteors.

I try to imagine what famous paintings I might have recreated on my house to get my own son home safely when he was lost in addiction. A rippling turquoise swimming pool by David Hockney? Or clouds of Rothko's colors, soft squares of fuchsia, scarlet? Picasso's dancing muses? A Rauschenberg collage that layers old newspaper articles, dead birds, photographs of the landscape, bits of broken furniture? Or a wall of neon color by James Turrell that slowly shifts from saffron to violet to cobalt? Would any of these have helped him find his way back to us?

Art and danger have always had an uncertain alliance. I have sometimes even tried to take it seriously when curators talk about a sculpture that is meant to make the viewer feel uncomfortable or an installation piece that is meant to "threaten" her idea about place or identity or something else. But honestly, when it comes down to it, who needs art to learn about danger? That information comes on its own, often and easily to all of us. I think those parents in Florida understood something far more real and profound about the value of art. It may be greatest when it makes the world a place that is recognizable to us.

Summer House

The minute I step into her house, I know I want to be her.
All the objects from my own house—the chipped ceramic
mugs, the worn floorboards, the photographs on the table
that are so familiar to me—I hardly even see them anymore.
They fade against the grace and solace I find in her rooms.

It is easy for me to forget who I am, to imagine myself
as some other when I am there. The floorcloths are painted
with stars, spirals, serpents; every knife in her rack is sharp.
The water glasses are cobalt blue, she has left home-baked
bread in the freezer for us, and in the early morning I listen to
the horn blast from the ferry as it comes into the harbor. She
has melamine plates that look *exactly* like used paper plates
with ants crawling across them. I wonder if it is possible for
me to *become* her. Perhaps all it takes is a view to the ocean
or a shower curtain that teaches me the names of leaves,
the American elm and American chestnut no longer familiar
to me, along with the Alaska fern, Monterey pine, shagbark
hickory, juniper, elderberry. I take ownership of all these things
in my effort to install myself into her life. And if I don't
become her, I imagine what it is to be her.

Which makes me wonder: Why is it so easy to assume the identity of someone simply by being in their house? And when so much of life depends on truly and deeply imagining the lives of others, why is it that this exercise is so easy to do in her house and so few other places? I am in a summer house for a few days in August, watching the sun filter through the arbor of wisteria leaves. Why is it that we are so often able to do things of meaning, significance, and consequence in the places and times it matters least?

Shreds

With the family dinner a thing of the past and national holidays often celebrated most ardently by sales at the mall, it's easy to mourn the disappearance of ritual in contemporary life. But what strikes me more at the annual shred event in our rural town is not the demise of tradition, but its unexpected and tenacious evolution.

The event takes place in the parking lot of the town hall. Constructed in the mid-nineties and sheathed in white composite clapboards, the building itself evokes an old dairy barn but in fact houses administrative offices, a meeting room, and the town court. Our gathering is a similar twist on tradition. We pull up in our cars and SUVs loaded with excess, but it's not agricultural produce. Instead we are hauling over bags and boxes of old tax returns, junk mail, piles of magazines, catalogs, newspapers, correspondence, legal briefs, bills, receipts, bank statements, and all the other detritus the digital age was meant to rid us of, but didn't.

The mobile unit, a box truck outfitted with an industrial-strength paper shredder, has pulled into the parking lot as well, and the graphics on its exterior state its purpose:

"The Identity Protection Program." And its abilities: "Paper shredding. Hard drive destruction. Media destruction." The message is reinforced by a gigantic image of a human fingerprint, that iconic emblem of our individual selves.

My own load consists of years of tax statements and financial files, old research notes, drafts, and manuscripts, and I dump it all into a wheeled bin that is then rolled over to the truck and mechanically lifted into the truck's interior where its contents are dumped and shredded. Sasha, the driver and Shred-Tech operator, invites me to look at the small display monitor mounted on the side of the truck. I watch as the blades grind my stuff into tiny bits. "Gone!" he exclaims.

The shred event is an occasion for strangers to chat with one another, as is the custom in such municipal assemblies. An older woman comes in with her old tax returns. "Usually I do my own shredding," she says to no one in particular. "Anything at all with my name and address on it." A guy in a red Nissan truck speculates that this is how the Mafia gets rid of people as he unloads all his dad's old police work into the bin. He has a Norwegian elkhound with him, gorgeous with its tawny and black markings, and tells me that he hunts bears and wolves with his dog. Wolves, I ask? In the Hudson Valley? He looks at me, bypassing the question. "Anyone comes onto my property, he'll rip them apart," he says, nodding at the dog and evoking an older and more primitive form of self-protection.

Sasha tells me that the paper isn't slivered into thin ribbons as they might be in regular office machines, but crosscut into tiny squares. "No way you could ever put it back together," he says. It's then sold to a local recycler, where it's baled for sale for other uses, mostly pulped for new paper products.

The event lasts a little over an hour. It isn't festive exactly, but most of us there seem to share a sense of accomplishment, pleased to be rid of our stuff. And it sparks a twinge of nostalgia. I've always thought of the barns in my area as a kind of architecture of sufficiency, but the sense of industry and the surfeit of material collected today at this faux barn isn't about storage or distribution. Instead, it's a kind of reverse harvesting; we've come with our surplus, but with the objective of obliterating it.

Still, we've convened in a time-honored manner, gathered in what's as close to a town square as we've got, to participate in a shared enterprise. And though it isn't meant to collect and distribute, but to reduce and eradicate, it's a service offered free to residents, a gesture of goodwill and one that encourages good stewardship.

Rituals remain a marker of community, defining our needs, reflecting who we are. It's probably as it should be.

The bad news is that what we have in common seems to be abiding fears of identity theft and the ever-multiplying excesses that are a by-product of the information age. If there's a shred of good news, it's that we are confronting these as a collective enterprise, something we can—weirdly—still do together.

The Ice Bar

I was in a bar once in Stockholm that was made entirely
of ice. All of it—the tables and stools, the shelves, the walls,
even the glasses were cut, molded, and sculpted from blocks
of river ice. Before we went in, my friends and I were asked
to put on thick, insulated capes made out of a textile with
a metallic reflective surface. As I wrapped myself in the one
handed to me, I intuitively assumed it was to keep me warm.
But of course, it was for the opposite reason: it had been
designed to prevent my body heat from escaping into the
room and melting the ice that was the building block for the
room and everything in it, all kept at 23 degrees Fahrenheit.

I knew the frigid room was nothing but a one-off—
a novelty, a tourist attraction—and that I looked ridiculous
sitting there in my silver cape sipping lemon vodka with
elderflower essence. All the same, I was incredibly happy.
I realized then that we do not necessarily need to have an
effect on the places we are in. The possibility exists that
we might even dress ourselves in ways that prevent us from
leaving our imprints in the rooms, houses, landscapes
we inhabit.

Preservation

I have a friend who does a fair amount of shopping at Goodwill. Recently, she came home with a two-dollar purchase, a rectangular chunk of clear acrylic inside of which was embedded a milkweed pod. The silken floss of threads and tiny seeds spilling out of them were dispersed in the resin just as they might be scattered in the air of a July afternoon. How did they do it, my friend asked in amazement. Of course I had no idea, but it reminded me of the "Miss Blanche" chair by the Japanese designer Shiro Kuramata, which we then looked up on my iPhone. It was made in 1989 and has little red roses that appear to float in the clear acrylic seat and sides. One of these chairs is in the collection at the Museum of Modern Art, while another sold at auction at Sotheby's for $409,000. The online listing also says that although the designer experimented with real flowers, the petals turned blue when exposed to the resin, so he used fake flowers instead. And then he realized that the flowers really *should* be fake, because Tennessee Williams's character, Blanche DuBois, for whom he was naming the chair, was herself fake. You may or may not agree with this.

I don't, but what I take even greater issue with is the disparity in the worth attached to these things. Because, honestly, the designer chair and the knickknack are not all that different. Both are expressions of fragility and weight; evanescence and solidity; transparency and opacity; the natural world and the synthetic world. If there is any difference at all, it is that the roses are just about conserving an object, while the milkweed has managed to freeze time itself.

Jury

My friend Elizabeth was recently summoned for jury duty.
It was a domestic violence case, and like all the other prospective jurors she was questioned extensively by the attorneys about whether she had ever experienced or witnessed such trauma in her own home. "No," she said repeatedly, "No, no. Absolutely not." It wasn't until she was driving home later that it dawned on her that she had lied. "I remembered," she told me, "that thirty years earlier my stepmother had shot my father, then afterwards, herself." Her father had lived, but her stepmother had not survived.

Elizabeth is a straightforward, honest, and intelligent woman, and she said she had not set out to lie in the courtroom; she was not trying to evade her civic duty. It was simply that she did not associate the events in her own family with the vague details of the case she had heard that morning, or even with the phrase "domestic abuse." Elizabeth had not been a child at the time; an adult, she had not been living at home. But in the courtroom that morning, these events had not entered her mind as she was questioned about domestic violence.

This makes sense to me. Maybe it is just an ordinary kind of disassociation that is common to how we organize information. It comes naturally to us to put the circumstances about our own family and lives in categories that exist independently, entirely separate and remote from similar, even identical, occurrences that take place in other homes, other places. Einstein said it himself: "We experience ourselves, our thoughts and feelings as something separate from the rest. A kind of optical delusion of consciousness." It comes naturally to us to view the facts of our lives as exclusive, distinct, particular—ours and ours alone. So much so that it is often impossible for us to recognize the sameness of the events in our lives. The strange thing about this optical delusion, though, that way we assign a singular place and order to our own experience, is that sometimes it is what enables us to survive, while at other times it can be the cause to unravel.

Decoration

I have always been curious about those people who stay, the ones who choose to remain at home during natural disasters, floods, hurricanes, wildfires, who do not leave home despite impending catastrophes and orders of evacuation. They have cars, access to the interstate, and friends two states away with whom they can stay. Instead, they hole up with their Labradors in an upstairs bedroom while waves from the hurricane flood the basement and wash the furniture from the first floor out to sea. They stay even as their cars melt, and hose down the roof shingles every hour while flames from the wildfires rampage through their neighbors' houses.

I am not sure that they are any braver than the rest of us. And I don't think it is really because they feel safer at home. I wonder maybe if it's more like the opposite, more like they understand some basic truth about the home as a place of peril. It's nothing to them that the roof has a leak or a bit of mold is creeping up the backside of a wall. Some experience or other has alerted them to the intrinsic danger of domestic life, and they are as attuned to the decorative possibilities of yellow tape and blue tarps as other people might be to textured muslin curtains and vintage linoleum.

Silence

When I was in my thirties, I lived for a time with a couple of cats in an apartment in New York City. The apartment was on the fifth floor of a brick tenement building. An older woman lived in the apartment beneath mine and we became friendly. One Sunday night after I had been away for the weekend, I came home to find a series of notes from her tucked under the door. Likewise, my telephone answering machine was blinking with a dozen messages from her. Read and listened to chronologically, the messages went from mild irritation to sheer fury. Would I please turn down the music! The cacophony of sound coming from my apartment kept her from sleeping, from thinking. It was torture. Why could I not respond to her various dispatches? What was the matter with me? And if I was unable to consider her comfort, could I not turn down the music for the sake of my cats?

I called her straightaway to explain that I had been away for the weekend and that the music could not possibly have come from my apartment. No, she told me, I was wrong, visitors in my apartment had played loud rock and roll all weekend at top volume. Only after a long conversation was

I able to assure her the sound had not been coming from my apartment but probably, in fact, from the apartment below her into which new tenants had recently moved.

Much later, a musician friend of mine told me that our auditory senses are susceptible to suggestion. And that when we *think* a sound is coming from a certain source or direction, that is what we *hear*. But such convictions, it seems to me, go beyond the auditory. Our expectations of noise, disruption, and trouble of all sorts can prevent us from identifying their true source, and the quiet certitude with which we honor our assumptions makes me think of my cats sleeping all weekend in that silent apartment.

Transom

Some friends of mine recently moved into an old house. It was built in the 1790s and has the simple, stark beauty that so many of these old farmhouses have. The front of the house had two doors, one a main entry that opened onto a hallway and another on the far side that opened to the kitchen. In renovating the house my friends kept both doors, but the door to the kitchen was simply preserved on the exterior of the house; the interior side of the door was concealed behind the wall.

I have to say that this disturbed me at first, the way the door seemed to exist outside but not inside. The arrangement seemed to convey some basic uncertainty about entrance, arrival, closure. For all its elegance, the fraudulent entryway got on my nerves, as things often do when you realize they are not what they seem. But still, I appreciated the beautiful exterior of the door—its deep brown polish, its impeccable hardware, its little transom window that you might imagine brings light into the room behind it, but of course doesn't because what this is not is a door. And the thought crossed my mind, then, that one of my friends in this house is a writer, someone who is familiar with ambiguity and understands that what is a door on one side can be a wall on the other, which was the moment I grew to admire this enigmatic and beautiful configuration.

The Screaming Tree

It is an autumn morning, and by eight o'clock I am on my
routine walk. With its shining white branches, vast canopy,
and ninety-foot height, the sycamore tree standing in the
meadow at the end of my road is a good destination. When
we moved here thirty years ago, my neighbor told me it
was a rare species that had been imported from the African
savanna. I believed her then but am no longer sure it is so.
What I *do* know is that we often build up elaborate myths
about certain features of the natural landscape to which we
are drawn. On this particular morning, the tree is alive with
sound. In fact, it is freaking out. It is screaming, all of its
bright leaves rampaging with noise. It is not the harmony
of early morning birdsong but a racket of rasping, rattling,
screeching; a chaotic and furious orchestra tearing up the
morning quiet. I know it is the starlings, hundreds and
hundreds of them, unseen, hidden in the leaves of the tree,
making this awful sound. The sycamore is not in agony. It
is just a lot of birds gathered here during their fall migration
in the branches of a tree, which on this morning stands as
a silent and immobile monument to that disparity between
what we see and what we know.

Ground

I have always been a water person. Sometimes, it's nothing more than a shower or doing the dishes, but running water aligns me. And if there is a lake or a pond or a river, or even just a swimming pool somewhere in proximity, it's about all I need. There is something about immersion, the texture of water on skin, the pressure of water that recalibrates the nervous system, heart rate, and circulation that brings me to life.

Which is why it is curious to me that in my living room I have a small collection of pictures of hills. It was unintended. I never set out to have these. God knows, they are not *curated*. The Japanese ink wash of low hills that converge with mist had belonged to my mother. A friend from Vermont used pastels to capture a cloud of yellow leaves beneath a rise. A watercolor by a woman I know depicts a hill close to where I live now, and its rise aflame with autumn trees is reflected in the pond below it. Another friend of mine spent a summer painting the hills of the Hudson Valley, and they appear as patches of soft colors at dusk—olive, taupe, lavender. I have two of these as well, one image the close-up of the other. And another is a small painting the size of a postcard, a vivid green hilltop scattered with trees, given to me by a friend who is a poet. In the short note that came with the gift, she wrote that it was by a Dutch painter who was in the resistance during the Second World War and afterward "could do nothing but paint tiny landscapes."

Looking at these images gathered together on this wall, these hills, slopes, and ridgelines in their improvisational arrangement, I realize they offer profiles of solid ground. They suggest some density of material, some stillness of earth, some permanent and fixed terrain that is a counterpoint to the fluid streams and currents that are so important to me. I realize, too, how easily the visual and experiential converge in our minds, but even more so, how varied the ways are in which we come to understand that we are shaped by place.

Acknowledgments

Thanks go foremost to Jan of Jan Hartman Books for her steadfast encouragement and support for this book. Her insights, thoughtful stewardship, and astute guidance for both the editorial and design facets of this book were essential to bringing it into being.

I was lucky to have Eric Karpeles, Ann J. Loftin, Kelly McMasters, Michael McTwigan, and Lisa Naftolin as early readers and am grateful to them for their generous and sound counsel. Jennifer Thompson at Princeton Architectural Press was wonderfully helpful—a discerning editor, an enthusiastic reader. I am indebted as well to Kristen Hewitt and Rachel Walther for their commitment to clarity and precision and to Laura Didyk for her impeccable eye. Thanks also to Benjamin English for his deft and sensitive approach to the design template for this book. Design director Paul Wagner worked with skill and sensitivity to refine this early sketch, and I thank him for that.

My immense gratitude goes as well to Aurore de la Morinerie for the drawings she has allowed me to use here. I have long admired the evanescent quality of her work, and it is a privilege to include some of it on these pages.

Individual essays in this book were first published
in slightly different form:

"Bric-a-Brac," "The Turf Hut," and "Air" first appeared
in *Lapham's Quarterly*.

—

"Exile," "Sofa," "Signs," and "The Room" first appeared
in *This Is the Place: Women Writing about Home*
(Seal Press/Hachette Book Group, 2017).

—

"History," "Furniture," "Bounce House," "Landscapes,"
"Music," "The Cracked Tile," and "The Screaming Tree" first
appeared in *Windmill: The Hofstra Journal of Literature & Art*.

Published by
Princeton Architectural Press
70 West 36th Street, New York, NY 10018
www.papress.com

ISBN 978-1-64896-150-2

Production Editor: Kristen Hewitt
Design concept: Ben English
Design and typesetting: Princeton Architectural Press
Illustrations: Aurore de la Morinerie

Library of Congress Control Number: 2022933271